ship shape

dorothea smartt

ship shape

PEEPAL TREE

First published in Great Britain in 2008
Peepal Tree Press Ltd
17 King's Avenue
Leeds LS6 1QS
UK

ISBN 13: 9781845230586

Peepal Tree gratefully acknowledges Arts Council support

dedication

For birthing me:

Ruby Elise Smartt
1927-2007
Myrna Ilare Dolores Bain
1939-2007

For imagining a writer's future for me when I couldn't:

Maud Sulter
1963-2008

To my inspirational godchildren: Jesse, Enkai, Chenjerai
(Jedhi), Mamadu, Saphia, Iyah, Lily, Daisy, and Kai
and the lovely Beko

Acknowledgements:

Earlier versions of some of these poems first appeared in: *Samboo's Grave~Bilal's Grave*, Peepal Tree Press, 2007; *Storm Between Fingers*, Flipped Eye Publishing, 2007; and in the journals: *Moving Worlds, JALA: Journal of the African Literature Association,* and *SABLE LitMag;* audio recordings on 'Poetry In Performance, Volume Two', and *www.PoetryJukebox.com*, www.57Productions.com, 2003.

Thanks are due to:
STAMP, the Slave Trade Arts Memorial Project and Andy Darby of Lancaster LitFest; Sue Ashford, formerly of Lancashire County Council Museum; Stephen Sartin, Curator at the Judges' Lodging; Melinda Elder of Lancaster City Museum; Hugh Cunliffe of Sunderland Point; Hugh Moore, formerly of Lancaster Maritime Museum; Kevin Dalton-Smith; and Alan Rice, Lancaster University.

AFFORD-UK, African Foundation for Development, for the commissioning of "Just A Part", 2003; and Martin, Beatrice, Brenda and Zack and other members and associates of The Iteso Welfare Association, Lambeth.

Poets: Kamau Brathwaite, Joy Russell, Sheree Mack, Cyril Husbands, Khadijah Ibrahiim, Patience Agbabi, Malika's Kitchen, Rommi Smith, and the legacy of Kwame Dawes' Afro-Style School.

Lubaina Himid, for her Judge's Lodging (Lancaster) exhibition, *Swallow Hard*.

Maryse Conde, for her novel *Segu*.

Larry Olomoofe, of the European Roma Rights Center in Budapest for sharing his article.

Ingrid Pollard, for her photo-work 'The Boy Who Looks Out To Sea' and for her curatorship of *Tradewinds – Landfall*, at the Project Row Houses and the Museum in Docklands.

Big thanks for the Texan hospitality of Project Row Houses, its staff, residents and children. With particular thanks to Sister Hamdiyah and T., whose class of the After-School Project affirmed Samboo's name as Bilal.

Carole Boyce Davies, for her diasporic vision and continued support.

Jeremy and Hannah for the miracle of Peepal Tree.

The continued loving support and belief of my extraordinary family-in-spirit: Jennifer Tyson, Ulanah Morris, Danny Abrahamovitch and Sherlee Mitchell. My god-brother Tim Fielder. My cousin Sherry Gibson, and my true-true friends, Adjoa & Jesse Andoh, Donna Weir-Soley, Delroi Williams, Michael McMillan, Raman Mundair, Kadija George and Jocelyn Watson.

The faithfulness and guidance of my eggun and ancestors known and unknown, and my supreme being in the Orisha, *Mojubá*.

contents

Just a Part

ruby lips

Dead men tell no tales,
but dead white men document plenty,
great tomes that weigh
over our living, African diasporic selves,
our living Black Mother;

while this Blackwoman peers at scanty facts
and barely sees anyone she could call family –
drifts into dreams
with the sound of a name,
the lingering scent of jasmine on the Underground,
the St. Lucy Parish winds unfurling something
she can barely name,
coming with memories greater than her own,
Ruby lips still whispering stories of family
even though she's gone.

So listen beyond the shallows,
there's wisdom to be learned through
fleeting words, instinctive feelings, thoughts
and inspired dreams, Olokun stirring,
sending dark bubbles from her depths
that are no more than air on the breeze;

those erudite manuscripts
that aid and abet,
corroborate and validate each other,
I will vilify with my mother's
knowing
sayings.

Samboo's Grave

a few words on samboo's grave

Sambo, any male of the negro race.

Brewer's Readers Guide

Sambo: A pet name given to anyone of the negro race. The term is properly applied to the male offspring of a negro and mulatto, the female offspring being called Zamba. (Spanish, zambo, bow-legged; Latin, scambus.)

E. Cobham Brewer, *Dictionary of Phrase and Fable*. 1898.

Sam'bo, n. [Sp. zambo, sambo.] A colloquial or humorous appellation for a negro; sometimes, the offspring of a black person and a mulatto; a zambo. <–deprecatory and impolite–>

Webster's Dictionary, 1913

Sambo: stereotypical name for male black person (now only derogatory), 1818, Amer. Eng., probably a different word from sambo (1); like many such words (Cuffy, Rastus, etc.) a common personal name among U.S. blacks in the slavery days (first attested 1704 in Boston), probably from an African source, cf. Foulah sambo "uncle", or a similar Hausa word meaning "second son". Used without conscious racism or contempt until circa World War II when the word fell from polite usage…

Online Etymology Dictionary; www.etymonline.com

My spelling of Samboo reflects its contemporary usage, and the Lancaster pronunciation of the day.

I was originally commissioned by Lancaster Litfest in 2003, to write a contemporary elegy for Samboo of Samboo's Grave. The occupant is an unknown African who died shortly after his arrival at Sunderland Point on the Lune River estuary of Morecambe Bay. According to the *Lonsdale Magazine* of 1822, he had arrived around 1736 from the West Indies in the capacity of a servant to the captain of a ship (to this day unnamed), at a time when Lancaster was becoming the fourth largest slave port in Britain. He is woven into the folklore of Sunderland Point:

> After she had discharged her cargo, he was placed at the inn... supposing himself to be deserted by the master, without being able, probably from his ignorance of the language, to ascertain the cause, he fell into a complete state of stupefaction, even to such a degree that he secreted himself in the loft on the brewhouses and stretching himself out at full length on the bare boards refused all sustenance. He continued in this state only a few days, when death terminated the sufferings of poor Samboo. As soon as Samboo's exit was known to the sailors... they excavated him in a grave... behind the village, within twenty yards of the sea shore, whither they conveyed his remains without either coffin or bier, being covered only with the clothes in which he died. (*The Lonsdale Magazine*, 1822)

See Alan Rice, *Radical Narratives of the Black Atlantic*, Continuum 2003; and
www.uclan.ac.uk/facs/class/cfe/ceth/abolition/sambo.htm;
Hugh Cunliffe, *The Story of Sunderland Point*, R.W. Atkinson, 1984, 2002.
and Melinda Elder's, *Lancaster & the African Slave Trade*, Local Studies No.14, Lancaster City Museums, 1994 (1991).

on sunderland point of the lune estuary

Samboo of River Lune estuary
cut off and submerged
under waning facts,
buried in Lancaster's memory
the myth of Sunderland Point
muddied with trade and profits
human sales
relentless waves of merchandise;
its shipping tides cut off and flood
far and near lives.

Locals say he came
off a ship, a faithful slave
to a captain gone to town.
Abandoned by this master
Samboo, stupefied, dies
and christian sailors with goodness
bury this poor heathen soul
on the shore where Sunderland
points to the highways of the open seas,
to ships returning from triangular trading.

shipshape & lancaster-fashion

The sailors burying Samboo knew.
They ensured cargo made the crossing,
keeping Africans tamed and able
for sale.

Sailors, singing a sea-shanty blues,
homesick danced on the decks, above
the deep choral undertow of African
voices rolling below.

The first time together,
new and old worlds prayed the voyage to end:
their brutish sailors' lives, the held down
terror of the submerged Africans.

Home in Lancaster, did they relate
stories to waiting wives and children?
Or were those ship's tales remembered
only when sailors shared a drunken haze

of rum-pint after rum-pint to soothe
them into forgetting our *Maafa*,
secrets kept to blunt disquiet,
a convenient forgetfulness.

untitled

He has no name but Samboo,
filled with your pity and remorse.
I wonder if this grave is empty;
because he's no-one, Lancaster can name
him for its past, not his people's,
bury him under its myths.

If he's there at all,
could Lancaster say his names?
Or would the accent slur to *Samboo*?
You thought you saw him.
Did he say his name was
Samboo? That's who you saw.

bringing it all back home

Here I lie. A hollow
Samboo. Filled with your tears

and regrets. The tick in the eye
of Lancaster pride. The stutter,

the pause, the dry cough, shifting
eyes that cannot meet a Black man's

gaze. Questions, questions from either
side that foul us for answers. The how

and the why ultimately defeating us
with shame, with anger, with the defensive

voices of those who lived and enjoyed
the benefits, who did not question too

deeply the source that enriched
all of Lancaster life.

Who will heal and elevate to light
the souls of your ancestors if

you refuse to remember? If you
cover their incarnations with half-truths?

Grocer? You were a Slave Trader!
And everything has its price,

and denial is only debt
with interest to be paid.

seven deadly sins of lancaster

Beware of fast tides
hidden channels and
quick sands
[A road sign on the way to Sunderland Point]

Pride: in Lancaster's swelling. In the purchase, enslaving of another human. (In their haste, they wave goodbye to the Meeting House.)

Covetousness: of phenomenal profits, great houses, civic largesse, and the high life. (The Lawsons, Satterthwaites, Rawlinsons, Dilworths, and Townsons at high-risk)

Lust: for grand returns on each voyage of *The Henry*, *The Swallow* and *The Sally*. (Dismissing their Quaker morals in praise of riches ushers in new days.)

Envy: of the untapped promise of other people's physical strength, yoked to work on plantations (to better their Lancaster high life).

Anger: fuelled with swelling fears of rebellion and loss. (Slow moving brethren protesting, not too loudly, so Lancaster could prosper in peace.)

Sloth: Quaker grocers, deaf with avarice, slow to respond to the Meeting House's questions, whatever the suffering of people found hung, drawn and quartered in slavery.

Gluttony: More, more, never enough. Each brigantine's bounty a grave of blood, lives swept away, like the misnamed Samboo, his body left in a field without a prayer.

pillars of the community

high seas
high finance –
low life

high command
high church –
low life

    high tea
    high ground –
    low life

high profits
high up –
low life

    high hand
    high standing –
high class   low life
low life
              high placed
              high note –
    high riding   low life
    high society –
    low life
             high born
             high court –
    high class   low life
    low life

             high table
             high priest –
             low life

             high class
             low life

high spirits high voices high light
             low life

high spirits high voices high light
             low life

samboo's elegy: no rhyme or reason

If I don't sing you
who are you?
Does not the word make the man?
— Maryse Conde, *Segu*

Lying at the site of Samboo's grave,
waiting for full earth to speak to me,
waiting for buried bones to whisper
as a flow of fears floods through me.

I'm held here at Lune River's estuary,
caught in fear, not daring to go down
again into the ship's deep belly —
the slaving schooner, moored off the coast,
its cargo-hold gasping with bodies
unable to stretch out. Heaving, I
breathe out; each heady in-breath a dream-
catcher, shipping me into the craft's
dark stench, weighted with irons, smelling
of vomit, sickly death of shit-piss
fear. The surging, billowing, rolling
never stops, and I bang! Holler! Cry out!
Moaning in my body *Let me out!*
Let me go! Sweating, as I reach up
in the black recess, I search for God.
Grip tight to that faith, like a light-shaft,
a slippery life-raft. *Merciful*
Aaa-llah, hold me! Merciful Aaa-llah
avenge me! Invoking old forces,
pagan ways, my ancestors, my expiring
neighbour! Anyone! Anything sacred —
Please spare me from this. Trial of

23

hopelessness, faithlessness, for months
no sight of land, only the world of
self-contained lashing brine, the ship on
foaming sea; men become beasts, bloodied
brutally beaten, raped, spewed on deck.

Lying at the site of Samboo's grave,
waiting for full earth to speak to me,
waiting for buried bones to whisper,
as a flow of tears floods through me,

poet, reluctant to reconnect, I
reach out, switch on my bedside light,
waking with terrors that will not leave me.

a sailor's life i

The shock of the newly press-ganged
at a sea-born baby tossed into the swell
by a hardened seafarer –
to his outraged gaze
the mate had simply mumbled:
Y'can't sell 'em.

Initiate, he'd flogged a shipmate
near to bloody death
and was then made to crap in his mouth;
broke rations of rum;
at the highpoint of the mainmast,
eye on the horizon,

the climbing told he was
a sea born-again man.

a sailor's life ii

And I, Quaker,
praying,

my broad hat under the turmoil
of stars
and I, slaver,

slaying,
my bright whip ripping a new soil
of scars

Kamau Brathwaite, 'Littoral'

A letter by the ship's captain
alarms me with its absences –
no horrors of his everyday,
no word of this to his ailing wife,
only his wishes to journey with her
to healing waters, Harrogate Spa.
He documents the minutiae
of his household,
while the ship is a void.
No storms. No shanties. No hollering
of the crew as they cast a black body overboard.
Only his Christian twenty, manning a brigantine,
with two hundred heaving Africans
incarcerated. Below.

the captain's wife's story

It was after a dinner with the West Indian guest,
agent from a plantation tied to my husband's ship,
that the dreams came and my soul's light
dimmed into dis-ease that poured out in fainting-
spells and anonymous pains of the body.

I began to fade. A fatigue from wrestling aside
an incubus – my loving husband
a slave ship captain, agent of the interests of
Lancaster's Quakers, now gross grocers,
their faith displaced by greed.

Now in the chiming of our crafted Gillows' clock,
I hear his ship's bell toll, enter an underworld
inflicted with anxiety and guilt.

The ship – my husband's ship – moored in blood,
dispersing merchandise into the Lune for our local
grocers' trade in slaves, merchants and seamen
spilling onto the quayside, fertilizes
the terrors of my nervous condition.

His hands and eyes hold me with love, the same
hands that strip the Negro of his flesh,
prise open, dig the enslaved's wounds,
stroking them with briny waters for discipline.

On our pilgrimage to curative mineral waters,
to heal me of my breach, I only bubble
with blood, keeping nothing down.

her cinquain chain

No moon
tonight – or you.
Only the scratch of pen
on paper, itching for you, my
longing.

Diary –
honest space for
confession? Pen, ink my
salvation? Each doubt and fear keeps
spilling.

Hands pause,
ev'ry nuance
blistering my fingers;
the harpsichord's mahogany
rasping.

Sugar
whipped, creamed. Fingers
licked. A prodigal's meal
from a West Indian plantation
cooking.

Hands stroke
tiny stitches,
my embroidered cotton –
fresh from the ship, by way of blood –
sewing.

99 names of the samboo

Bilal
ibn
beloved
son
brother
husband
father
grandfather
kin
elder
ancestor

sold
livestock
cargo
chattel
property
guinea-bird
savage
enslaved
captive
servant
worker

heathen
cannibal
beast
blackamoor
darkie
nigger
uncivilised
wog

fuzzy-wuzzy
coon
negro

tamed
eunuch
pet
uncle tom
minstrel
golliwog
survivor
mirror
mask
chameleon
creole

signified
dehumanised
damned
vilified
debased
silenced
invisible
camouflaged
trickster
caliban
signifier

threat
animal
oversexed
terrorizer
buck
bull

breeder
raper
lynched
rhygin
rebel

warrior
bussa
cudjoe
leader
toussaint
revolutionary
guerilla
cimarron
subversive
cuffy
duppy-conqueror

outsider
illegal
other
criminal
refugee
foreigner
exile
uprooted
immigrant
sojourner
hyphenated

prodigal son
garveyite
rasta
nubian

kushite
nation
fulani
blood
progeny
family
Bilal

eclipse over barbados

Look up man! Wha wrong wid d'moon?
D'sky clear-clear, an' a t'ousand stars flickering,
begging me look up. Dey are endless!
But wha' happen to de moon? Man she slipping 'way!
Cast over by sumtin', blot out, the dark rejoicing!
Disappearing, she staring eye interrupted! –
Is dis m'las chance to run 'way?
Get on d'ship?
Not get on d'ship?
How I is to read dese signs and portends?
How I is to know? She slipping 'way
but look, she peeping out de nex side,
coming back to me, whole I hope.
Maybe she got secrets fuh tell me
when I cast m'full eye pun she.
Moon? Wha' could mek y'pass yuh dark side pun we so?
The waiting ship?

Dey gon put me in the deep-down hole again.
An' all I could do is let dese quiet tears
fall and shake m'soul-case heavy.
Mek me dig m'hans in dis earth to keep me here.
The others, here to stay,
look pun me like I doom, like I is a traitor to leave dem.

I leavin? Or somebody takin' me?
It's not fair! Dey doan like me, 'cause I leavin,
leavin d'pickney gang;
leavin de steaming pot of molasses
and de hard-wuk cane, and de licks;
leavin de sun brooding down on muh back
searing de sores an' de scars from d'whip.

I leavin dem to boil in de rum factory,
to mash and tun, to be mash and tun.

I leavin
an' de dark moon telling me t' g'long
an' see what pun de other side.
Mebbe d'ship gon tek me back
Mebbe d'ship gon tek me back!

An' Mummy will be dere, pounding cassava,
an' Daddy will sing out a call to prayer jus' fuh me,
jus fuh me one.
Maybe.
Maybe.
An' dis disappearing moon? Dancing slow widda shadow,
whu she got t'tell me?
De full-shine o'she marking my face
with signs. There an' then,
there an' then, she made me her own.

An' I know
how much she want me back,
and I goin' on dis nex ship
and maybe,
maybe, jus' maybe,
it gon take me home.

my calling

I tell dem
my name is
Bil'...
Bill, they reply,
Right you are,
young Samboo,
Bill it is.
Dey laugh at
me. And I
keep de source
of m'smile
hidden as I
whisper to
m'self – yes,
yes I is my
father, the muezzin, son; I is
Bilal.

My true-true
name
is a secret
I keep from those
that would de-
file me.

stars in my heart

I reach m'fingers in de air
reach fuh d'stars, way up dere.
Draw 'em down, so bright, so smart.
De' will lead m'home, from inside m'heart.

a boy 'whose faith is sure'

*"...and the difference of night and day... and the ordering of the winds,
are portents for a people... whose faith is sure..."*
Surah 45, Al-Jaseyah 1-37 (*Quran*)

As dawn expands over a distant horizon,
across the cerulean blue of the Gulf waters,
Bilal summons his faith to pray

and home is just a heartbeat away.
The ship's shape streams through,
making waves dolphins crest,

gliding alongside. He is afloat
in a calabash of mysteries, the deep unknown
below, above the azure heavens.

Signs and portents of the glassy seas
are puzzles and riddles to a small boy.
The winds caress the memory of his mother's voice,

and he is at home with the sea-salt aroma now
buried in his skin, but deeper still is the smell of her
as she feeds love that reaches him

up high on the brigantine's mainmast,
square-rigged sails curved taut with wind.
He remembers that prayer is better than sleep

and hopes this new voyage, these new men, will take him home.

kiss

Memories are smoke
lips we can't kiss
hands we can't hold...
                    Kamau Brathwaite, 'Prelude'

Absorbed by night,
still stars in the breeze
become friends. Bilal
lifts his eyes to rub stars
together, sparking visions
lettering the sea.
His long sighs
become ships to ride;
waves breeze-blown
lift the sails of memory;
mind and senses slip.
A gust picks up power,
a full wind, hot
on his ears – harmattan dust,
his mother's lips on his neck-
back – whispers love:
Home is always waiting for you.

observant

Watchman watching:
bowed body braced in the pre-dawn,
the cautious boy bleating
his blues on deck, ears cupped,
listening on the wind, then
hands on knees, smelling salt
on the planks and again,
Subhaana Rabbiyal A'ala,
Subhaana Rabbiyal A'ala,
Subhaana Rabbiyal A'ala.
Allahu Akbar.

The sailor sees him
at moonrise, standing straight
then spreading low into a stretched sprawl,
fluid, flexing face-down, forehead falling.
Piteous palms pressed on planks,
he glances to his right then left, lips trembling,
bleating across the baleful blue,
palms wiping a solemn face.

a long way from home

Sailor
Waves, rise, roll
me home, salt
skin, salt breath.
Heave-ho sail!
Trust stars, trust
wind before
horizon
to push me
homeward to
Lancaster's
cold grey seas.
Heave-ho! Sail
swell; waves, come
roll me home.

Bilal
Salt m'skin
salt m'hair!
Heave-ho sail.
I cyaan trus'
win', blow so!
I cyaan trus'
betray-me
stars, drag-me-
'way grey seas
that push me
'way t'dis
Lank-cush-ster.
Heave-ho! Swell,
roll me far,
teef me 'way.

lancaster keys: the brew room

Sunderland points to West Indies plantations.
A Samboo, like Gillows' crafted mahogany,
is farmed and forested, torn from root
systems to harden or die,
to be shaped into something new
and of use to Lancaster Town.

Sunderland points to the new home
for a Fulani, Bilal, called Boy (no matter
his age) by his owners,
their primrose path paved with mahogany
bodies. Fallen nature. Hardness
of heart, shameless water courses.

The ship's crew gave their cabin boy
a name: Samboo. Like he didn't have
his own old father's family line,
names respecting Allah, the
One, Allah the beneficent, the
merciful, names that speak of a
way paved with his ancestors, each
name an elegy, a praise song.

A Samboo — a converted life,
fed just enough to confiscate its labour,
and disposable as an animal past its use;
Lancaster keeping the harvest, fermenting
a homesick bitter brew — a Samboo
kicked from his calabash pot.

A desolate breed lashed from
the shaft of his life-source,
trapped by distance and isolation,
their Samboo pines for his master, mythical
imagined key and centrepiece of his world.

I see this Samboo, this boy Bilal
in the Brewery room – outpost
of a West Indian estate – away from the boiling
reek of molasses for rum,
pining for the familiar, where rooms are many,
in one dwelling, in one
compound, in one village, in one
land, in one kingdom, in one
empire, in one continent.

A fermenting homesick brew, he drains out,
kicked from his split calabash pot.

the present arrives

Husband

Good wife, he wrote, *it troubles me you are alone,*
while I voyage for so long. I bring you something to ease
your hardship, and comfort your days. It will no doubt
amuse you, remind you of me, and be the envy of the local ladies.
Home at last, with this strange Samboo,
he expected her to smile, warm to this gift like a Caribbean breeze.
But she turned paler than the insides of the coconut he'd shown her.
She, primed with news that had travelled ahead –
Something dark this way comes! –
whispered finally through the silence
pregnant like a Quaker meeting:
Get that thing out of here!
Then came her screaming, and brown Bilal's eyes opening wide.
The Captain reached for her hand. Her recoil heaved his heart.

Wife

This black-skinned boy,
eyes wide and white on me!
Take it out of my sight, I whisper.
It is blinking! Husband,
do you pretend to love me?
What gift is this that hurls me into your present?
I am no senseless London lady.
My insides run against me,
sweat shivers, my body gives way.
The dark boy's eyes stare,
so black he is a shining nightmare.
A gust of sugary saliva rushes my mouth,
my avoidance defeated and suspicions alive.

Bilal/Poet

He waits, stabled with horses
until a man takes him inside the less-than-grand house.
The Captain will call him through a closed door,
and he will enter as planned. He waits outside,
for the familiar voice, white servant nervous beside him.
The door opens on a woman with straw-thin hair
that she scrapes back with pallid fingers. There he is,
ill-fitted and costumed in somebody's second best. He looks
to the Captain, but sees him take her hand, ready to comfort,
while the other flaps, fanning an order to exit.
But he cannot move,
his tongue twists, untwists, and twists again.
So with his lips he grins, exposing his teeth,
hoping to make the Captain's lady smile.
Shirt sticking to his back, her howling hollering in his ears,
Bilal senses his end in her screams.

bilal's cinquain chain

Cap'n
took him from the
house back to the *Ship Inn*.
More waiting. Bilal thinks, *Where to*
now? Home?

Tools for
a brew in place,
fermenting in the room,
Bilal lies asleep. Until they
arrive.

The door
opening swabs
him in light; curious
peering faces bathe pale in his
blackness.

He sings,
lost in wilful
words. He never knew song
could soothe his sad soulfulness, keep
him whole.

Downstairs
dancing for the
wide-eyed locals, up on
the bar, sailors bang a jig for
Samboo.

the door locked

And I stood
like a plank,
staring. Door
locked. D'room
did not move
swell, sway like
d'ship. Small
window give
light. I could
see d'ship
still on quay.
Captain had
not said tie
me. But d'
innkeeper,
innkeeper
look at me
an' see a
devil ting!
I know he
frighten a'
me. I know
it. I could
a' laugh – but
I know that
fear from de
plantation,
from d'man
overseer
eyes, Master
deh eyes – he

looks could kill
yuh! He fear
could kill yuh
stone cold dead.
D'rope tight,
I try to
undo m'
tired hands.

because i'm nothing you can name

"...I still do not exist because the 'me' that they see is one they have constructed without my participation..."
Larry Olomoofe, *Visible Invisibility:*
Deconstructing the Hungarian Gaze

You despise me
before you know me,
recreate me as something of your own,
and don't stop to ask me.
I don't think, therefore
I'm some thing you can toy with.
I'm nothing, to be made some thing
useful for you to examine, fill, classify.
You assume I am yours for the taking,
presume I was just waiting for you
to make me mean something.

Because I'm nothing you can name
I become nothing,
expire when you leave the scene,
a shadow cast from your light.
I'm nowhere, the edge of terra incognita.
I'm nothing, the unknown incarnate.
I'm nothing, your antithesis, your anti-Christ.
The chimera on the edge of your map,
something to be tamed, domesticated
and you call me Samboo.

Because I'm nothing you can name
I scare you. You war against me,
decide I cannot live.

As I lie down I slowly fade,
pine and expire, defaced and denied,
saddened and alone in your world.

Because I'm nothing you can name,
I repeat my own names to myself –
Bilal Amadou Ibn Sori –
over and over, out loud. I let them sing in my ears,
bounce off the perimeters of my confinement,
define me, Fulani, beyond your stares,
anchor me in the quicksand of my memory,
call up echoes of home-voices sounding
my true-true names, with love.

Because I'm nothing you can name,
I falter in my eyes. I peer at my reflection
at the quayside wondering
if my mother will recognize me?
Am I still my father's son?
Are my grandfathers ghosts?
Am I still alive at home?

Because I'm nothing you can name,
I no longer speak, my words senseless,
and you hear nothing. I swallow myself
whole, haunting my insides.
I look for a way out.
I am not brave, I do not offer resistance;
I am not wise, I have no answers and questions disappear.
Because I'm nothing you can name,
I am not.

shut away

Sitting pun ole sacks
facing d'shut door,
light and noise
come up tru' d'floor
boards, under d'straw.

Pacing d'room to an' fro,
I hear de men downstairs
talking 'bout the Samboo.
I listen fuh d'Captain voice,
but he's not there.

I look in a cupboard,
see ole dusty kegs, barrels
like de ones dey on the ship.
To an' fro, pacing dis room,
'pun new lan, d'ship homeland.

Not my homeland.
What I is to do here?
Where d'gon send me now?
I keep m'ear to d'floor,
keep m'eyes on d'door.

mama's bangles

Sounds like a bell —
Mama bangles pounding yam,
Timbuktu tinkling
in my Uncle, the young Imam, gift to she.
Bangles like nobody's in the village,
bangles that ring out
where she is to clay-faced men
before they took me. Perhaps
she still living, still
at home looking fuh me?
Hol'ing out she palms to rub m'head,
an mek she bangles chime?
Perhaps she in Allah paradise
or she wid d'ole gone-before-people?
Lef' t'one side fuh d'magic markings of Allah,
were d'ole Gods angry, like our fathers said?
Did they send the clay-faces? Did they
send me 'way from Mama to punish she,
me, we? I miss my mama,
but want she here with me to wuk de canes?
To tek d'lash?
To run wid she han's all between she legs
from d'whiteman, to chime in wid d'night screams…?
NO! NO! That would be all wrong!
They woulda treat she like a beast.
No. I glad she not here wid me. Glad,
I cry at the sounds like a bell.

in the upper room

I frighten to shudder into the drum,
frighten fuh de rhythm riding m'body;
no way will I succumb,
let drum song shiver through m'ears
echo through me, mixing in m'hips.
Where the drums come from?
Not from dem sailors downstairs,
or d'hands of that innkeeper, or from d'quayside,
outside. Is from m'inside, deep,
seeping from m'toes,
taking me home, to other feet pounding,
exalting in the beat.
Still I frighten, but I let my pelvis lean
into de drum. Where it gon take me?
I travel, I travel and d'drums keep on,
bringing sweat to d'side of m'neck.

becalmed

Windless   moon   frozen;
he is quiet on the outside,
within stagnant and muddied.
Pool of cold night sky:
light dying   deep blue   stolid.

dis-ease

The calabash of his life half-spilled
and emptying out,
with each fearful thought
dark clouds come over and,
just to keep it halfway full,
he counters each cloud with a hopeful retort.
Perhaps it will help them blow over.

The doubting duppy is there,
tearing at his life, calling back slurs
he won't answer,
can't answer.
He sleeps and hopes the jinn will be gone
when he wakes, but
it follows him.

Dreams of anxiety wake him in the morning;
the friendly guinea fowl turned into a vulture.
.

blues under the moon

Sinking lower into misery,
sleep's his favourite place to be.
The moon's the eye of the sky
seeing him blue.

His heart's a ton of lead,
his eyes are playing dead.
The moon's the eye of the sky
seeing him blue.

His tongue's like a stone.
The only sound he can make is a moan.
The moon's the eye of the sky
seeing him blue.

His mind is unglued,
can't focus on what else to do.
The moon's the eye of the sky
seeing him blue.

Stripped by the force of apathy,
every past mistake had a curse to leave.
The moon's the eye of the sky
seeing him blue.

Awash with worry and woe,
mired, he's no place to go.
The moon's the eye of the sky
seeing him blue.

His legs want to shiver,
carry him down to the bottom of the river.
The moon's the eye of the sky
seeing him blue.

Full moon's the eye of the sky
seeing him blue.

Full moon's the eye of the sky
seeing him blue.

a few words for samboo

Bilal, a Fulani son,
unwilling, unconsenting sacrifice
to Lancaster town's transformation from wood
to gleaming Georgian stone, Lancaster city,
each rising white house a gravestone,
with window eyes, half-closed
to the far-off shore of screams.

And their ships kept leaving for more.

ballad of the ship inn
(*loosely to the tune of Greensleeves*)

On Sunderland Point, at the mouth of The Lune,
is where you'll find the Ship Inn's...

The trade was good, as it should be
with all the brigantines in
but this was a boon, the Captain's coon
in the brewery room of the inn.

On Sunderland Point, at the mouth of The Lune,
is where you'll find the Ship Inn's...

The curious came, the old and the lame;
cider, ale and rum she flows,
his pockets well lagged, the innkeeper brags:
I'll better any travelling show.

On Sunderland Point, at the mouth of The Lune,
is where you'll find the Ship Inn's...

From all aroun', from Lancaster town,
come see a sight as rare as gold,
for the price of a brew, hear tall-tales from the crew,
and the strange Samboo you'll behold.

On Sunderland Point, at the mouth of The Lune,
is where you'll find the Ship Inn's...

Upstairs in pairs, one by one if you dare,
you can take a more private look,
to marvel and coo at the lad's head of wool
or touch his black skin on tenterhooks.

On Sunderland Point, at the mouth of The Lune,
is where you'll find the Ship Inn's...

You might giggle and point, he won't disappoint.
Some matrons even moan, *He's just a boy*.
They'll bring him gifts that the innkeeper shifts;
that shrewd landlord's overjoyed.

On Sunderland Point, at the mouth of The Lune,
is where you'll find the Ship Inn's...

Tallow candles light the deepest of nights
as he led them up with an air of doom –
at his blackness men cursed, could the devil be worse! –
to what was in that room.

On Sunderland Point, at the mouth of The Lune,
is where you'll find the Ship Inn's...

See the Ship Inn's show, a once lively little curio,
this Samboo a Cap'n did disown;
in some kind of trance, still for the sailor's he'd dance
and his mumbo jumbo he'd moan.

On Sunderland Point, at the mouth of The Lune,
is where you'll find the Ship Inn's...

Hale and hearty he was at the start,
but then the lad seemed to lose heart.
He'd to earn his keep, no one's fault he woan't eat!
But there's nowt to be made from viewing a grave.

On Sunderland Point, at the mouth of The Lune,
is where you'll find the Ship Inn's…

Come by day or by night, for a price here's a sight
you can say you've seen a man's shadow cast.
He's not to be missed, though now motionless
he's still our Samboo, while he lasts.

On Sunderland Point, at the mouth of The Lune,
is where you'll find the Ship Inn's coon.
On Sunderland Point, at the mouth of The Lune,
is where you'll find the Ship Inn's coon.

bilal's daydream or tales of ibn bilal

He is his father's son.
Prodigal, he returns,
hero, adventurer,
returning from the fringe
of the white cloth, upturned
edges of the Calabash.
Masha'Allah!

From the ocean's deep space,
a rolling galaxy,
warrior of the seas,
he's branded and stained.
He is faith, unafraid,
devoted muezzin.
Masha'Allah!

Though the stars are displaced
he could not be broken;
he is Ibn Bilal,
his scars are his trophies.
His new beard is grown long.
He returns a new man.
Masha'Allah!

His mother knows him,
though his brothers do not.
He stands like a fortress,
his tormentors undone.
He is his father's son.
He is strong in his faith.
Masha'Allah!

Who will believe his tales
of tall canes breaking men;
massa's ships breaking men;
prison island's labour,
man woman child labour;
but he unbroken, though a boy!
Masha'Allah!

The moon, eye of the sky,
saw Bilal, spoke to him
of home, the last prayers
of the day, his mother's
voice waxing and waning
through his suffering trials.
Masha'Allah!

Cosmic winds danced their dance,
as on land, as at home,
kissed mountains and oceans.
Though the stars were displaced,
he had faith. He strode on
Allah's way. Unafraid.
Masha'Allah!

The floating night-star, slim
then full, faithful sister
in the ocean of night,
flirted with the cloudscapes
indifferent to his songs:
He submitted to God.
Masha'Allah!

Signs and wonders beheld,
he came to understand
the language of their ways.
Shifting villages rose
and sank in tidal waves.
He stood like a fortress.
Masha'Allah!

Ibn Bilal returns!
singing voices chime. The
compound of his father
sounds with Allah's praises.
His name's remembered, now
and forever, Bilal.
Masha'Allah!

He is his father's son.
Prodigal, he returns
hero, adventurer,
returning from the fringe
of the white cloth, upturned
edges of the Calabash.
Masha'Allah!

at sea

Seas criss and cross into confusion,
the night-glow lights the waters –

a dark shining hide,
swelling high, plunging low.

How many full moons pass
with the sting from the sea's sons?

Ancestral spirits, come!
Find him, take him home.

Sails, hunchbacked,
swinging on the wind,

carry the lost words of his name.
In this seaworld, he's another boy.

today on sunderland point

The boy who looks out on Lune Estuary calls;
tradewinds moan through boughs of beached schooners,
sucked into tidal muds; both longing for a ship
to sail, heading with the reeling birds, home.

just a part

aubergine angels

Inside Old Street station,
I meet my Waterloo:

Aubergine Afros, primed,
shining and armed, wrestle

my gaze from briefcases,
from city zombies' eyes;

the sweating on the back
of broad builders' T-shirts;

a small boy's arms running
with ice-cream; a bacon

sarnie in the happy
mouth of a homeless man.

Arrested by the sight!
– the light of grander dark

halos moving me up
and out. So I exit

to City Road behind
young Black boys. Black angels.

front room angel

"...The West Indian Front Room [exhibition] created an emotional response amongst visitors because it offered a means of recognition and identification of material culture..." Michael McMillan, curator

christmas charm bracelet i got that morning
big sister watching   I beg to wear it
all day even after Mum left for work
saying   *put it up before you lose it*
yuh could tek off d'bracelet now dahlin'

and it was only after lights were out
and yvonne and me talk and play and talk
in our bunk beds i know my wrist empty
we turn our bedroom up-a-side-down
me looking more wild and scared than yvonne

i'd be the one to catch licks   terrified
of what daddy would say and then do me
stinging under mummy hurtful silence
she'd already been vex about working
chris'mas night   daddy was angry with mum

tell she how the hospital doan like blacks
mum said is not only coloured people
working tonight and kiss she teeth at him
we made the best of it and had dinner
earlier daddy had walked her to work

me and yvonne had forty minutes home
alone to watch our telly   we switched on
mr & mrs and left *songs of praise*

our four rooms feeling empty without them
radio times in hand we plan the night

no matter what on when daddy came back
he wanted to watch sophia loren
in the big film   she or 'lizbeth taylor
d' only two white women worth their salt
we giggled   he had sophia loren

picture paste inside one of his books
the little stars on the tree glittering
i pull open the red velvet curtains
mummy had put up special for christmas
it wasn't real velvet but who could tell

i let in the stream of yellow street light
through the lacy net curtains made whiter
by the dark shadows living in corners
fairy angel at the top of the tree
balancing like a drunk man on one toe

the small coloured lights of the christmas tree
sparkled in the corner   white   silver   gold
plastic-strip-tasselled branches bent open
from the box   surviving another year
pretty glasslike balls mirror the front room

cold   daddy in bed   teeny white dot gone
from the telly   screen in the corner quiet
making the room spooky   mummy not back
till morning   daddy clocks loud in the night
but now nothing will chime till quarter past

midnight   i creep to our settee gold arms
leatherette icy to the touch   i push
my hand down the side of orange cushions
my chest shrinking from the chill coming through
my new pink frilly brushed nylon nightie

nylon didn't do much to keep off cold
i wished i could put on my new bright blue
dressing gown but the threat of being branded
a *new niggah* kept it folded and wrap
up in the clear catalogue plastic bag

this new pink nightie was from last christmas
brought out specially for this special night
our new slippers   our usual present
last year's were long gone and we had waited
were okay to wear so my feet were warm

underneath was a old *radio times*
i find a thrup'nee bit   yvonne watching
me wave it at her   but she couldn't see
both arms full i lift each seat one by one
she at the door waving at me *hurry!*

i can't see it   too much noise to turn chairs
upside down to poke through torn holes we'd made
to the treasure-trove corners at the base
settee's cotton cloth black-bottom hiding
things that drop down the back   like my bracelet

soft soft i move about   blonde hair   blue eyes
making her beautiful   the fairy sings:
wait 'til the dark night is over   why should
your heart slip away   when the dark midnight
is over   watch for the breaking of day...

she had sent me a message   the fairy
voice soft as an angel   have faith and keep hope
telling me i'd find it in the morning
believe god in his wisdom would answer
my prayer like daniel in the lion's den

yvonne an me had search all we could search
and it was up to the fairy angel
to be a true messenger of the lord
and for me to be a true believer
i fall asleep and had a lot of dreams

just a part: a distant lot

My family are a distant lot.
Some I've met, maybe once,
many never at all.
I do not know their likes or dislikes,
I struggle to recall their names.
They do not surround me
at significant times of the year.

My family are a distant lot.
Their faces do not spring to mind,
I do not see shared gestures or
ways of saying.

My family are a distant lot,
scattered around migratory paths: from Barbados
landing up in London, Birmingham, New York,
Panama City, Nassau, Miami, Havana.

My family are a distant lot,
people whose names I write down
to remember, interrogate my mother
to make connections on paper –
my family extending across the page –
great uncles and aunts on their travels.
Mum remembers letters arriving
in Bridgetown with news of babies born,
cousins to know.

My family are a distant lot.
Cousin Sherry and I, excavating names,
make mention of a place
with the same address in Bridgetown.
Her grand-aunt's board-house is my grandmother's,
its sole occupant now the grand-daughter,
providing a link for scattered family.

My family are a distant lot.
Sherry and I find each other, cautious,
each behind a video camera,
smiling at our visceral need to record,
sitting in a room of her family, my family
of not so distant cousins.

For the first time,
at twenty-something, in a room full of
faces holding familiar fragments
of my mother, my sisters, my own,
here, in this living room, I see
my cousin smile my mother's smile.
See her mother's long fingers equal my own.
With diverse kin extending around the room
my sense of self opens out.

This one time we meet – maybe never again –
I ask their likes and dislikes.
Ask them to recall names my mother told me.
As they surround me, aunts become sisters-
in-law, uncles become fathers.
Faces spring from old photos; I see
shared gestures and hear our ways of saying.

My family and I are just apart.
And this distant lot are just
a part I could not see, do not live around.

And I wonder if blood is thicker than water,
even when the bloodline's vague and unknown.

And I wonder if the family I'm born to
is the family that will make me whole.

a roomful of feeling

I walked out the door
moved out   took my suspect self
to a place where I could think the possibility
took a coach to Amsterdam
outside family and prying friends

to ask myself how much
of a woman was I going to be.
Would I make do with a man
or open the door on a roomful of feeling?

loving women

It's a dangerous joy,
well-travelled all the same
in spite of threats.
We have been here before
hidden in stories of back-home
Caribbean women, *more than frens.*

My father knew, my mother knows,
of women *like that*
telling no names –
is only after she gone
her childhood friend tells

of our *macommère* Great Aunt
living with she *fren.*

just a part: remittances

It's what keeps people 'back home' going –
family ties and our longing for 'home'.

An older sister, she did her best from over here,
sending pocket money and small packages.

First she takes on her sister's children;
not just the boarding school fees, but the uniforms,

towels, bedclothes, paper, books and calculators
so easy to find, so inexpensive – not like at home.

When she transplanted herself to Milton Keynes
the shape of love and family grew to barrels

full of 'River Island' end-of-line clothing;
stories of her whole village dressed bring a smile.

just a part: sacrifices

A text message beeps,
riding the packed bus from work:
"wen can u sen £".

Like phonecard talk-time
it's money for medicine,
money you will find.

Talking to your twin,
eighty minutes for three-pounds –
this phonecard is good –

sacrifices you,
an older sibling, make to
benefit the young.

Here you are. Fam'ly
beyond these British borders,
a part of bloodlines,

diaspora lines,
weave you in a world wide web
of phonelines, airlines,

money-transfer lines.
Pounds fly home quicker than you
could get there. Back home's

always in mind. Home's
time of day, rates of exchange
you know, like your PIN.

heart and feet

My toes curl. I watch for her breath,
smell death. On the ward bed,
heart-red stain at her mouth,
she is still. I see her toenails, red

like mine. I did them last night.
Let me go out with style, she said.
The screen's a flat red line,
a lone tone the nurse turns off.

My heart. It slips out my feet,
stains a smudge on the clean floor.
Can I ask the nurse to fix this?
You gave me my heart to love with,

my feet to move through the world.
A ring of coins around your toes,
a toll for the gate,
soft red earth and leaves at her heels.

litany of survivals i

There's so much left. The bedsit full
of barrels, bags and boxes packed to go;
Like a bondhouse, Mum sighs. We arrive
early morning, edge our way round piles,
Mum and I, stare at all Cousin Iris' things.
We begin to sort and share out decades
of shopping that never made it back home;
packs of panties, bulk rolls of j-cloths,
boxes of soap powder, bottles of cleaning fluids,
packets of tea, bags of rice, cups with saucers,
plates and bedclothes, buttons, zips, and balls
of edging lace, fabric by the yard, multiples
of the same dress, shoes, watches, T-shirts:
all piled up ready to go. Waiting for shipping,
or to be carried by the next body going home.

Her West London funeral was a family affair.
A sparse sermon noted her years of generosity.
Cards were read from overseas. A good friend,
together with Mum, would see a headstone was placed.
Her brother, cinnamon eyes darkened with shadows,
sweetboy years behind him, locked in a marriage
to a Jehovah's Witness wife and child
(a road refused, *fuh a good glass o' rum wid de fellas*),
curdled at the warehouse store, pleading:
Pass 'em on t'somebody that could use 'em, nuh!
Mum promised to make sure what was needed
finally made its way to Barbados cousins,
whose faded blue-sky envelopes, folded,
preserved, dated through the decades,
left with me for the last bus home.

litany of survivals ii

There's so much left. The wardrobe's
full of time past, and times to come
without you. Under your bed is packed
with suitcases you'd asked me to clear,
older brown grips of your arrival
replaced now with seventies beige
vinyl cases, navy-blue eighties,
crowded with good buys kept
for yet-to-be days. Knitted nylon
blankets you gave to us *macommères*
at Christmas, not quite his'n'hers but still
matching; English rose tea-sets set aside
for guests; hand-me-downs laid to rest
by bargain clothes; the sewing machine
lost among rails of ready-to-wear;
armchair-back covers, in a world of sofas
irreverent to Sunday best;

your first passport, royal blue, corners cut,
stamped redundant, packed behind bursting
white louvred doors that murmur
hopes for a useful future. Mum arrived,

packed the wardrobes, to leave them full.

red mudder

When the message come thru
Daddy first woman gone,
I couldn't help thinking how she outlive he long.
She was a cord to he pas' life, he life before me,
a young fellah 'bout Bridgetown circa 1933.

Not long after he pass, I went out to meet her,
ask she all 'bout Daddy –
and any memories that keep her.
She pass way now and all she stories gone
but the Red Mudder did pass summa dem on.

The Red Mudder, common-law,
tell me all 'bout Daddy young boy days,
the fella she fall fuh, the kinda faader he made.
She still had the 'Singer', but he goat long gone.
Even one o' she dawter dead, lef' she an' gone long.

Daddy was a man like nuff women –
so she tell me, as we went 'long!
But she feel she was he red queen,
and with he mudder on the scene,
she was not like dem others at-all.

She bring out de ole Bible, where he write up
all their children names –
the Bible sen from London,
widda picture of he 'bout Town,
pidgins bustlin' 'bout Nelson's Column
and this Bay Street boy. See
he really arrive now!

Then there was he old passport pic –
he, widda moustache, I never see that yet!
She, in she good-dress, mek up the night before –
it had a red sash, and small red bows.
De hat was de ting – Daddy sen it from London (de Motherlan')
and de dress she make to match.
Lives they live before I even hatch.

When the message come thru
Daddy first woman gone,
I couldn't help thinking how she outlive he long
She was a cord to his pas' life, he life before me,
a young fellah 'bout Bridgetown in 1933.

old spice man

Old Spice! Man,
the roll of the sea
carrying you back home,
your ashes lining a coconut tree.

Old Spice man!
The schooner on the bottle
like ships that held us in the hold,
our red screams above the deep.

Old Spice man –
Dad, meticulous in tailored suits,
cut sail to suit the winds of change,
his mother dead, not left behind.

Old Spice man
had me in his mellow fifties,
shaved of wild youth and slim moustache,
your voyages internal, into the man
you'd been, the sage you hoped to become.

Not a *Lawyer-Boy* now! People
call you a new name. Old Spice man
is a *Obeahman*! – *Oh sweet mystery of life,
at last I've found you!* –

Old Spice man!
Rolling in the depths of Olukun's chest,
surfacing in a next generation.
Surfacing in me.

shango daughter birthday

Ojo ro mi O, you should see she dance d'Shango!
We could feel d'riddim-roll, deep down in her soul
O Jaja ra la – beat d'drum too bad, karele...

Streets with sheets of rain,
a day of cackling crimson thunder,
storms as Silvia speeds from the Savoy Hotel
across the slate of the Thames.
The sun sets, saffron on deep fuchsia
candy floss streamed across the noisy horizon,
while among the leaves on the South Bank,
the quiet blue lights glitter with magic.

The white-clad woman throws her body into
the rhythm, dragging thunderbolts to the ground.
This is a Bembé! You should see she dance d'Shango!
It's Silvia's first birthday, no wonder there was a thunderstorm
over Loughborough Junction. *Sango de I de, Sango de I de...*
In the deepening darkness we see
the Italian daughter fluent in Shango macho walk,
Sister Honey Dee witnessing signs and wonders,
so that today, tomorrow, and the days after she'll feel
a London night beckon with batás beating, bells
dancing in her heart. Shango raised up,
draped in scarlet velvet, on a birthday throne,
batás beating in a Brixton basement.
Best to go without, so you can have it all!

Iya Mase lobi Chango, Iya Mase lobi Chango.
Bobo araye oni kuele, Iya Mase lobi Chango
Bobo araye oni kuele...

Batá drums singing Port o'Spain, New York, Miami, Matanzas,
Ile-Ife into the humid low-ceiling spot,
even as the torrent of colours of Cuban faces –
African, Asian, European and all between – mix
in a Brixton night, to sing praises to the old Gods.
Caribbean sista-fren at hand offers up eloquent Italian
praises – declaring the language better suited to the passion
of the batá's bells dancing rhythms in a British basement,
for Silvia's first Shango birthday:

Ojo ro mi O, you should see she dance d'Shango!
We could feel d'riddim-roll, deep down in her soul
O Jaja ra la – beat d'drum too bad, karele,
Bobo araye-oni kuele
Ojo ro mi Shango!

notes

p. 18: *Maafa* ('Shipshape & Lancaster-fashion') – a Kiswahili term for 'disaster' or 'terrible occurrence', used to describe the African Holocaust of the trans-Atlantic slave trade and its consequences.

p. 20: *Grocer* ('Bringing It All Back Home') – a contemporary Lancaster misnomer for those involved in the buying and selling of goods from the so-called 'West Indies trade', the trans-Atlantic slave trade.

p. 27: *Lancaster Quakers* ('The Captain's Wife's Story'): Those who ignored Quaker condemnation of traffic in slaves as unchristian included the Lawson, Rawlinson, Birket, Satterthwaite, Miles Townson families, all Quakers, all slavers; from conversation with Stephen Sartin, Curator at the Judges' Lodging, Lancaster, 14/7/03.

p. 37: *Subhaana Rabbiyal...* ('Observant'): "Glory to my Lord, the Most High (x3), God is great" a refrain from Salat , the daily prayers.

p. 41: *Gillows* ('Lancaster Keys: The Brew Room'): Working out of Lancaster, Robert Gillows was known for his innovative use of mahogany, a popular wood imported from the West Indies. The company later evolved into the world-re-nowned Waring and Gillows – *"Robert Gillow's success as a merchant in the West Indies trade had provided the substantial financial backing to enable his company to prosper".* Judges' House Museum, Lancaster.

Fulani: The Fula or Fulani are a nomadic people of western Africa. They were the first group of west Africans to convert

88

to Islam; historically they are the missionaries of Islam. As such they would sometimes come into conflict with other West African peoples. See, Patience Sonko-Godwin, *Ethnic Groups of the Senegambia: A Brief History*, Sunrise Publications (The Gambia), 1985.

p. 61: *Masha'Allah* ('Bilal's Daydream or Tales of Ibn Bilal'): Pronounced "Ma-shah-Allah", meaning "As God has willed": a phrase used when admiring or praising something or someone, to avert envy and jealousy, and in recognition that all good things are blessings from God.

p. 70: *The West Indian Front Room* ('Front Room Angel') *The West Indian Front Room: Memories and Impressions of Black British Homes*, 18 October 2005-19 February 2006, Geffrye Museum, London. One in a series of site-specific installations by Michael McMillan, showing memories and recollections of migrants' front rooms. www.thefrontroom.org.

p. 77: *MaCommère* ('Loving Women'): a French creole word widely used throughout the Caribbean generally meaning "my best friend and close female confidante" ['About the Name', Helen Pyne Timothy, *MaComere: The Journal of the Association of Caribbean Women Writers and Scholars*]. Less sexually explicit than the synonym "Zami(e)", a French creole word, often used to derogate [rather than celebrate] being "...in a sexual relationship with another woman". Richard Allsop, *Dictionary of English Caribbean Usage*, OUP, 1996.

p. 86: *beat d'drum too bad....* ('Shango Daughter Birthday'): Adapted from Sparrow's calypso, 'Shango Man', from his LP, *Sparrow at The Hilton* ('67 Carnival Hits). Trinidad AR NRC8070; and from Ella Andall's 'Karele (Let's Go Home)' from her CD *Sango Baba Wa* © 2004, Music Organisation of Trinidad and Tobago (634479527319).

Bembé: a drumming, singing and dancing ritual party in Santería, at once functional and festive, marking some important event in the religious life of a devotee or priestess or to celebrate a particular orisha. George Brandon, *Santeria from Africa to the New World: The Dead Sell Memories*, Indiana University Press, 1993.

Sango de I de...: From Ella Andall's, 'Sango De I De (Sango Has Arrived)'.

batás: a Santería ceremony with batá drums is generally known as a bembé. Three batá drums (small, medium and large) are played simultaneously to create polyrhythmic compositions, or "toques". They are decorated with bells. The double-headed drums are shaped something like an hourglass, with one end bigger than the other. They are used primarily for religious ceremonies by worshippers of Santería in Cuba, Puerto Rico, and in the United States. They originate, as does the religion, from the land of Yoruba, in Nigeria.

Bobo araye oni kuele: Afro-Cuban folksong from Santería/Lucumí tradition in praise of Shango, that also praises his mother. Roughly translated: "Mother Mase, gives birth to Chango... The people come to welcome him".

Ojo ro mi O...: Adapted from Sparrow's calypso 'Shango Man', and Ella Andall's track, 'Jaja Ro Mi / Oju N'ro Mi? (I'm Homesick, Sango)'.

praise for **ship shape**

'From the slave who is robbed of his family names to the love that dare not speak its name, this book is a penetrating quest for identity. Its strength lies in a multitude of voices transporting us to the core of Bilal's slave narrative and the poet's own personal history. Well researched and often punctuated with refrains, it leaves us wanting to know more.'

Patience Abgabi, Poet.

Dorothea Smartt has in a way cool-down from her tierce - her fierce - 'Medusa Poems' (**Connecting Medium**: Peepal Tree Press 2001) and has now deepen in towards Family (the second seQuence of her new poems here) and widening out towards the recovery of his. tory & her. itage in the Sambo Poems of the first seaQuence, whose central poems 'The Captain's Wife's Story', 'Her Cinquain Chain', 'The 99 Names of Samboo' and the bell-wrought Caribbean narratives of her second heart *("Best to go without, so you can have it all')* are destined for the world's anthologies

<Kamau Brathwaite in October New York 2008>

'In blues-y, well crafted poems of loss, and desire, *Ship Shape,* uses the sea as its controlling metaphor in order to get to the difficult history of past and contemporary migrations. Its strength is its reclamation of the legendary "Samboo" from degradation and an end on the lonely and bleak Lancaster shore to reinstall him in African Diaspora mythology. The troubled slave trading history of the British is revealed by these means to be the genesis of today's African Diaspora in the U.K.

As Smartt provides a mother for Bilal, she imagines his

dislocation, aloneness, loss, separation from family, she also gives him the life, bones, flesh and blood to facilitate this recovery. This then is counterpointed with the poet's own reading of her family, her own losses, and new understandings of being "just a part" of a much larger story. Along the way are wonderful intertextual connections with another Bajan writer – Kamau Brathwaite – the well-known poet of the "crossing". Dorothea Smartt reveals a poetic intelligence and maturity of form and content which definitely locates her among the best of her generation of poets.'

Carole Boyce Davies
Cornell University

'The trauma of the Trans-Atlantic slave trade still echoes across the diaspora today and the poet Dorothea Smartt in her new collection *Ship Shape* shares with us what she listened to of those whispers, wails and cries for freedom. She excavates the un-marked grave of an African boy buried at Sunderland Point, Lancaster. He was supposedly called 'Sambo', as Dorothea tells us in 'Because I'm nothing you can name, I become nothing.' Like an archeologist Dorothea invokes the spirit of this young boy by creating an identity, family, history, culture, religion, a home for him. He becomes Bilal, a Fulani Muslim boy and she inhabits his body, his soul, his mind as he becomes a survivor of the triangular salty 'Maafa' from West Africa to Barbados to Lancaster, where he comes an exhibit, a novelty for the bemusement of the 'Pillars of the Community' in Lancaster town. *Ship Shape* is an ambitious collection that resonates from the page long after reading it and it has a visceral poignancy.'

Michael McMillan, writer, playwright, curator/artist
of *The West Indian Front Room*

also by dorothea smartt

connecting medium
ISBN:9781900715508; pp. 72; pub. 2001; £7.99

'*Connecting Medium* links the past to the present, the Caribbean to England, mothers to fathers. Here are poems about identity and culture, generations and the future. A powerful sequence of poems about a black Medusa. Poems that link the material world to the spiritual one. Poems that recreate a sixties childhood in South London in vivid detail. *Connecting Medium* is full of energy and life. Hers is a bright, passionate voice.' – Jackie Kay

'As Caribbean Woman move into the oras of their own consciousness, wonderful new icons emerge to join Gort, Tacky, Zumbi, TL, Galahad & the Midnight Robber - Tia, Fola, Harriet's Daughter, Sister Stark and the Mary's: Prince, Seacole, Wiggins, Wages, Yellow Mary, MaryAnn of the Shifting Sand, GypsyMary and Mariana Grajales, to welcome a few.

Now for the first time we havin a Dread Mary. The Black Medusa of this new voice in Caribbean poetry, this Brit born Bajan international, is Dorothea Smartt, who will tangle you up & burn you to stone

Here she is
standing ready
to rip to claw to beat
you to your monster self.
Narrow the focus
block the light.
In your own tall shadow
crouch quiver whimper.
Let your hair grow long. Rage
down to skin and bone. Rage
red-hot-blue-cold
tearing you. Solitary in the dark.

And that's only page 65' – Kamau Brathwaite

about the author

Dorothea Smartt, born and raised in London, is of Barbadian heritage. Her work as a poet and live artist receives critical attention in both Britain and the U.S.A. She is acknowledged as tackling multilayered cultural myths and the real life experiences of Black women with searing honesty. She was Brixton Market's first Poet-in-Residence, and a former Attached Live Artist at London's Institute of Contemporary Arts, and a Guest writer at Florida International University and Oberlin College, U.S.A.

Dorothea Smartt is a working poet, with a wealth of experience as a creative writing facilitator and mentor. She is also poetry editor of SABLE Litmag, and co-Director of Inscribe, a creative & professional development project for Black & Asian writers. Described as "accessible & dynamic", her work has been selected to promote the best of contemporary writing in Europe today. Dubbed 'Brit-born Bajan international' (Kamau Braithwaite), her first poetry collection *connecting medium* (2001, Peepal Tree Press), is highly praised as the work of "...A master artist who sculpts both Standard and Caribbean English into a variety of poetic forms... capable of boldly crossing cultural boundaries" (*Caribbean Writer*), it also features a Forward Poetry Prize 'highly commended poem', and includes poems from her outstanding performance works "Medusa" and "From You To Me To You" [An ICA Live Art commission]. She's read and performed as a live artist, both nationally and internationally, and enjoys going into schools. Her next installation [video/poetry text] will feature at the Museum in Docklands, London as part of the international exhibition "Landfall" in February 2009.